The Victorian Elver

Time of Trial

This book is a walk through time - a time of elvers past, when the little beast rode the Severn bore in such huge numbers, that fishermen of the night saw by Lantern and flame, what seemed a great serpent passing endlessly before their eyes. In those far off days people were few, the elvers many.

It is the story of those country Severnsiders harvesting the welcome springtime arrival from time beyond memory. Taking their lowly share, and wanting no-more.

And how the changing years brought those country people to the streets of Gloucester City, and ancient laws were dusted off, denying them their precious fishing rights.

Such laws brought forth defiance, and moved the Victorian Government of Country and Empire to hold an inquiry at Gloucester itself, which gave back the elver to the common people.

All this happened long ago, and as we tumble into an uncaring 21st Century-those Severnsiders with long memories, regretfully wonder if the little beast has a future at all. For these days people are many; the elver few.

Published by
REARDON PUBLISHING
PO Box 919, Chelenham, GL50 9AN
Tel: 01242 231800 Email: reardon@bigfoot.com
Website: www.reardon.co.uk

Written and Compiled
by
William Hunt

Layout and Design
by
Nicholas Reardon

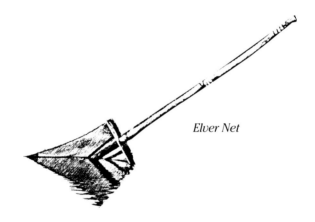

Elver Net

ISBN 1 873877 82 X
ISBN (13) 9781873877821

Drawings
by
David Ochiltree

Printed by
Stoate and Bishop
Cheltenham

Time before Trial

Thinking back to times when life was less complicated, and more rustic, it's easy to imagine the small working Severnside populations of past centuries, elvering to their hearts content, reaping the spring harvest in secluded peace; free at all times from official interference. And the fact is, you'd be dead right. They did just that.

England was generally not quite so merrie however. The game laws threw their long shadow across the villages and hamlets of England, on both land and water. Not so long ago, the petty sessions of the old country courtrooms, were filled with poaching prosecutions.

Invariably, the magistrates came from the landowning class, and those charged with poaching offences oft found themselves judged by the very magistrate on whose land the offence had been committed.

The census returns of Gloucester prison 1871, give a snapshot of the inmates and their prior employment. Agricultural labourers are in good attendance throughout. [1]

1. 1871 Gloucester prison census.

However, elvering on the Severn escaped the attention of the authorities, which was odd, because on paper at least, a battery of Acts had outlawed the pastime along the Severn for centuries past.

1533- Parliament of Henry V111 prohibited the taking of elvers for ten
years. 25 Henry V111, chap 7   2a

1558- Elizabeth 1 made the prohibition permanent. 'For the
preservation of spawn and the fry of fish'. 1 Elizabeth 1,
chap 17   2b

1667-The Act 30 Charles 11 chap 9. 'For the preservation of
fishing in the river Severn' absolutely prohibited taking 'the
fry of eels, commonly called elvers', the penalty for such an
offence being 5/- and the forfeiture of fish and nets.
2c

1778- Things eased somewhat as The Act 18 George 111 chap 33 was
passed, repealing certain parts of the Act of Charles 11, and
allowed people living on the banks of the Severn and Vyrnwy, to
take elvers for their own consumption, but not to sell.
2d

Statutes aside, however it seems that nothing was ever done to enforce
these laws. The earliest reference we have of an elver net so far is from
an inventory of a Thomas Pyrry of Blaisdon taken 22nd September 1587:
'In woode and timber an elver nete'. By then, elvering had been outlawed
for thirty years, but Thomas Pyrry didn't seem troubled. [3]

The local historian Rudders, wrote in his book 'New History Of Gloucester
shire 1779', that, 'elvers are cooked as white as snow, and brought to local
markets, where they are sold at 2d a lb'. This was taking place just one-
year after George 111 Act forbade their commercial sale. [4]

A century later, elvermen of some fifty years standing testified before the
1876 Gloucester inquiry - and none could remember anybody ever being
prosecuted for elvering before. Even the inquiry officials admitted, that in
spite of extensive searches undertaken, no records of prior prosecutions
could be traced. [4]

So that's how things had stood, since time out of mind. Though placed on
parliamentary statues, the laws had never been enforced. So how comes
this anomalous situation?

Well; I think its best at this stage to look at who were the law makers.
They were of course the Landowning class, and these people naturally

viewed complete dominion over fish and fowl as an absolute prerequisite of landownership. If it moved it had to be owned, and the elver as a recognized seasonal river visitor, could not be excluded.

After all; was not the Severn also passage to the 'king of fish', the salmon, and the much prized lamprey - as well as being home to abundant marshland fowl? Perhaps night time elvering could be a ruse to poach at will.

Having gained dominion over the little beasts in law, the landowners found they had no further use for them. One look at these wriggling disgusting, wormlike creatures was proof plenty that the poor and the elver were meant for each other. The dining tables of the Lords and gentry were host to all manner of fish and fowl from their estates. The elver- never.

And when they turned up, there were millions of the things, so what then? Moneymaking opportunities were dismal. The only people who ever showed only interest in them were poor labourers and peasants, and they never had but a few coppers to spare at the best of times.

As to poaching fears; the elver arrives on the sweeping high Severn tides of March and April. The spectacular rise and fall of water levels, with its accompanying waterborne debris of logs and branches, effectively rules out fishing for anything else. On the lower Severn too, the main salmon and eel takes come later in the year.

So the elver harvest was left to the labouring poor, who in their turn eagerly awaited the springtime coming. After a hard winter, a sackful of elvers for the pot, kept the family in body and soul for days at a time, and any surplus could be sold for ale money. At this time of plenty, poaching the landowner's estates simply wasn't necessary.

The elver at this time might stand comparison to blackberries today:

A seasonal event, occurring in great abundance-having little financial value-picked from the hedgerow by an ordinary person - completely overlooked by the hedge owner.

Events for once conspired to favour the poor: Timing of nature, - class distain, - and paltry profitability, ensured the Acts remained in disuse.

Generations of Severnside dwellers continued with their seasonal take; totally untroubled by laws that were never enforced, and of whose existence they knew nothing at all.

Alas' It couldn't last forever. These Acts had been burning on a very slow fuse, and finally after centuries of neglect, the statutes were dusted down, and the authorities for the first time began to look at their workability in good earnest.

The Severn Fisheries Board

The Severn Fisheries Board came into being in 1867, and was one of a number of Fisheries Boards formed at the time. They were set up in response to the findings of an earlier Commission investigating the sanitation problems of towns and the disposal of the waste therein. [5]

Among other things, the Commission had recommended that salmon rivers be protected from sewage pollution by a system of local control and conservancy; and that these measures be set up nationwide.

The Severn Fisheries Board's jurisdiction ran from the higher reaches of the Bristol Channel along the whole length of the Severn itself, and took in the catchments tributaries, and rivers that ran into the Severn, including the lower Avon at Tewkesbury. Especially important were the vital upper watercourses in Wales where the salmon spawning beds are located.

The policies of The Severn Fisheries Board were in service to the protection and well being of fish in general, and the salmon in particular. It was self-financing, meeting costs by issue of fishing licences, raising rents and levying fines, as well as receiving donations from its members on the 'Board of Conservators'.

So who then were the officers and members of 'The Severn Fisheries Board?' At its heart, it was a roll call of upper crust English society of the day, comprising of peers of the realm, landed gentry and civic dignitaries.

The Severn Fisheries Board itself was divided into county districts, through which the Severn and associated waterways ran. Each county district elected and returned county members onto the Board.

Where the Severn flowed through a City, namely Worcester and Gloucester, then City membership was included, giving the local council dignitaries, and other town worthies; usually the mayor and alderman, the chance to join the Board and rub shoulders with the Toffs.

As well as elected conservators, there were also the honorary or 'ex officio' members, and these included the more substantial landowners whose estates bordered waterway courses under Severn Fisheries jurisdiction.

Below Gloucester both Lord Fitzharding of Berkelely, and Sir William Vernon Guise of Elmore Court were examples of ex officio members, and this state of affairs was replicated throughout the county districts. Although not elected, they had access to the Board regarding pertinent matters, and for advisement purposes.

Finally there were a tiny number of representative members, which consisted of fishermen or fishmongers themselves. These hands on types were useful in providing direct information as to the business end of the fisheries.

Because of the great length of the waterways and the diversity of the environment to be managed, the Severn Fisheries Board held its AGM at different venues along the Severn itself, which included Gloucester Worcester & Shrewsbury, giving with any luck, all interested parties throughout the huge catchments area, a chance to participate and get a hearing.

However the heart of the Board and its administration lay at Worcester, and was overseen by Vice Chairman, 'John William Willis-Bund' who resided at 'Wick Episcopi Estates', located just below Worcester and bordered by the Severn and Teme.

John William Willis-Bund was born in 1843, and his commitment to civic duty was beyond question. By 1873 he held three posts on The Severn Fisheries Board: Vice Chairman, county member and representative member. His father John Walpole Willis also Wick Episcopi was an ex officio member.

When not attending to matters relating to the Severn Fisheries Board, Willis-Bund was also JP for Worcester, and later became Chairman of Worcester County Council. Possessing an LLB degree, he was able to practice as a Barrister.

The Severn Fisheries Board was a new broom, and under the energetic auspices of Willis-Bund's office, a certain management view began to form. A policy emerged, whose origins can be traced back to the Worcester membership itself. In the year 1873, this policy was formulated into law, and ultimately brought consternation, and disorder to the banks of the lower Severn itself.

The Ban

The Seventh Annual General Meeting of the Board of Conservators of 'The Severn Fishery District' was held 16th September 1873 in the Guildhall Worcester.

The Officers of the Board were as follows:

Chairman
The right Hon Lord Northwick

Vice Chairman
J. W. Willis Bund Esq. Worcester

Treasurer
John Swinton Isaac, Esq., Worcester

Clerk
Mr. Henry George, Guildhall Worcester

The meeting began with breaking news. It was announced to the gathered conservators, that the 1873 Salmon Fisheries Act had passed through Parliament, and was now law. Preparations were to commence, for the implementation of the Act, in the following spring of 1874.

(Traditionally 1st Sept to 1st Feb was salmon fishing close season.)

On the face of it there was nothing very remarkable about this announcement. There were always salmon laws. However nestling within this 1873 Salmon Act was a crucial section 15, which unusually dealt with eels, and even more remarkably - elvers. It was very brief, not much more than a paragraph and the text read:

'That no person between the first day of January and the 24th day of June inclusively, shall hang fix, or use in any salmon river any basket net or trap, or device whatsoever, for catching eels, (or the fry of eels), or place in any inland water, any device whatsoever to catch or obstruct any fish descending the stream'. [6]

Well what does that all mean? If you were an eel man, it meant nothing at all. This section is saying in essence; don't let your eel traps interfere with salmon descending the river between 1st Jan and 24th June. The eel man sets out his wing nets to catch the outward migrating eel shoals in the autumn; nowhere near the dates mentioned.

The other main Severnside method of trapping eels is by use of a putcheon, (traditionally a wicker basket pot). These are baited and set down on the riverbed, and do not interfere with salmon at all. If they did, they would have been outlawed hundreds of years before. The eel and salmon inhabit different environments within a waterway system, and require separate fishing techniques to catch them.

In fact section 15 exempted the putcheon, and it could be used, between 1st Jan and 24th June as long as the diameter of the trap entrance did not exceed 10 inches diameter. So the eel man was unaffected by the new Act, and could carry on as before. [6]

The crucial five words are, 'or the fry of eel', and the dates 1st Jan-24th June inclusive. As the elver arrive in the spring months, this effectively prohibited elvering along any salmon river in England during these times.

So finally after centuries of official indifference the Severn Fisheries Board set about enforcement of this new law, empowering its water bailiffs to take action against those out fishing; and if necessary, the police could be called upon to give assistance.

Yet although a national law, it was only along the banks of the lower Severn that it was ever enforced. So what then, had brought about the dramatic change in official perspectives, upsetting as it did the long held status quo? The answer can be given in one word -Gloucester.

Whilst the rural Severnside parish population levels generally remained steady, Gloucester industrialized and grew rapidly. People quit the countryside and flocked to the towns and cities at this time.

Gloucester And Sample Severnside Parish Populations

	1801	1831	1851	1871	
Ashleworth	476	540	590	564	
Sandhurst	365	434	494	602	
Gloucester	7,718	11,935	16,015	16,223	
Elmore	381	401	374	430	
Frampton	860	1,055	983	856	
Arlingham	506	744	693	566	[7]

By the 1870's Gloucester had become a busy place. People teemed and swarmed within the old city boundaries; families were large and mostly poor. These west-end population densities packed tight to the very rivers edge, would be all too eager to avail themselves of the elver harvest.

The attention of the conservators may have been further drawn to another worrying aspect of burgeoning Gloucester fishing activity. No less than the course of the Severn itself, parting as it does above and below Gloucester.

The meadows bounded by the two channels give us Alney Island. For the elvering fraternity, it was just a hop and a skip over Westgate Bridge to get there. Once on the Island, they had the choice of two watercourses at their disposal.

To those concerned officials, it may have seemed that the elver was fished twice over, and by more nets than ever. In the event, the Severn Fisheries Board had come to the conclusion that the elver was being hit hard before it could get any farther upriver, and drastic controls were now deemed necessary.

For the poorer Gloucester people, who dwelt along the banks of the Severn, many had no voting rights, so when the law forbidding the taking of elvers sank in, no political redress was open to them; but they had a few cards to play, not least a strong sense of indignation, leading ultimately to defiance.

John William Willis-Bund Portrait: Ref 899 701 BA 8415

In the end these Gloucester people answered not to the Severn Fisheries Board but to the factories and commerce of an Industrial Gloucester: 'The Atlas Works', 'Moreland's Match factory', 'Gloucester Wagon & Railway Carriage Co', and 'Gloucester Docks', all employed hundreds of people living close to the Severn. Forelock tugging to the Squire just wasn't going to happen.

Whether the Gloucester conservators present at Worcester that day grasped the implications of section 15 is doubtful, for as the 16th Sept meeting drew to a close, Mr Jenner-Fust (Gloucestershire), proposed a motion, seconded by Alderman Riddiford (Gloucester), to resolve unanimously: 'That the special thanks of the Board be tendered to their Vice Chairman Mr Willis-Bund, for his laborious and able exertions during the progress of the 1873 Salmon Fisheries Act, through Parliament'. [5]

Events were leading towards a remarkable scenario. The country landowning Institutions were to attempt to enforce game laws on an industrial workforce, over which they ultimately had no control. Town and country were on collision course.

Loopholes

The insertion into section 15 of the fateful five words 'or the fry of eels' had implications that nobody had foreseen, and when the Act came into force, it was found to be deeply flawed. In certain places on the Severn, it was soon discovered that this law could be easily circumvented.

The commercial waterways that locked onto the Lower Severn were a glaring case in point: Sharpness, Lydney, and Framilode basins all operated at floodwater in order to move craft on and off the river.

In the spring, masses of elvers would flush through these lock gates, especially so the new huge basin, constructed and opened at Sharpness in 1874, providing an easy take for those with buckets and rope. It was that simple.

Once inside these artificial waterways, the elvers ceased to come under the jurisdiction of the Severn Fisheries Board. Dockworkers and boatmen hauling in the live booty on company premises could stick their fingers up to a watching but powerless bailiff. Almost certainly, any complaints made to the authorities would fall on deaf ears. They were in the business of shifting commercial tonnage, not conserving elvers.

At Gloucester docks however, the rope and bucket trick was not a practical option. Here at the canals most inland point, the Severn is narrow, and on the rivers east channel, a strong current drags past the lock gates at all times. On big tides, the gates, (then as now) would be closed to shipping, effectively shutting out the elver shoals from the main docks basin.

A further cause of frustration at Gloucester end might be gauged by an article that appeared in CITIZEN, MAY EDITION 1886. The article noted, 'quantities of elvers were taken to Birmingham in sacks'. Possibly the cargo ran up the waterways.

Prior to the railways, an internal elver trade must have grown up along the canal. In all likelihood, elvers taken at the lower basins, were shipped up to Gloucester docks and transferred to the waiting narrow boats bound for the midlands.

At the time of the ban, it's quite possible this super-highway kept elver supplies moving upriver. If so, it must have greatly annoyed those Gloucester men working the wharfs, and bereft of elvers themselves.

For the natural waterways, as with the canal systems, the same state of affairs applied; whatever flowed or was washed into another waterway system, that was not a salmon river, was beyond the remit of the Severn Fisheries Board.

The Frome, and the Leadon, are just a couple of examples where elvering could technically legally continue; in fact just about any culvert, inlet or pill was fair elvering game - but what about the Avon's confluence with the Severn just below Tewkesbury? It was definitely a salmon river, and as the Fisheries map shows, the Board's Authority ran up to Evesham.

At this time Tewkesbury had a single county member on the Board of Conservators, and this was the Mayor of Tewkesbury himself. On 21st Feb 1874, the Tewkesbury Register gave notice that under section 15 of 1873 Salmon Fisheries Act, elver fishing was banned.

But as far as I can ascertain, no prosecutions against the taking of elvers were ever made along lower Avon banks. The whole thrust of the prohibition, was clearly focused on the lower Severn, - and Gloucester was in the middle of it all.

And so the spring of 1874 dawned, and with posters and handbills festooned along the lower Severn banks informing people of the ban, the magistrate's courts began doing brisk business in unfamiliar territory.

The 1874 Court Cases

First off the mark happened to be two Tewkesbury men, Joseph Hathaway & James Walker, summons on 2nd April 1874 before Tewkesbury court:

'For having on the 23rd March last, at Deerhurst, in a salmon river called the Severn, used an elver net for the taking the fry of eels'. [6]

Worcester bailiff William Huxley issued the summons, and Mr Henry George, Worcester clerk to the Severn Board of Conservators, brought the prosecution.

Interestingly the bench thought that it an open question as to whether the elver was actually the fry of an eel. Mr George stated that if they had any doubts, the Act of George 111 did not, and furthermore if he'd have known the question was going to be raised, he would have brought Frank Buckland down to prove it. In the event the magistrates found in favour of the prosecution and fined the defendants with time allowed paying.

Joseph Hathaway   Fined   1/-   costs 10/6d   (57p)
James Walker   Fined   1/-   costs 10/6d   (57p)

Then: 12 pennies (d) = 1 shilling or 1/ - and 20 shilling or 20/- = (£1).

 A farm labourer's weekly wage was 12 shilling or 12/- a week   = (60p).

On April 25th 1874, seven men were brought before Gloucester court charged with the taking of elvers.

Magistrates on the bench:

Edmund Halliwell   Beachamps Lodge.
Rev Baker   Hasfield Court.
Captain De Winton   Wallsworth Hall.

The accused were: Henry Hewlett, George Ansell, Henry George, Jo Edwards, William Wyman, Bill Roberts and Bill Tongue. [8]

Acting for the defence was a Mr Chessyhre from Cheltenham. For those men in the dock, hiring a brief would have been a costly business, and it's doubtful they could have afforded it. By coincidence, a certain Mr Francillon was present in court. Influential Gloucester personages were taking an active interest in the proceedings that day. [9]

Mr Willis-Bund speaking at Worcester shortly after the trial, confirmed outside involvement in the dispute. It appeared that a sum of money to the tune of £100 had been donated by a number of persons to fight the elver ban. Mr Willis-Bund added, "that these combinations must be defeated". [9]

At the court hearing itself, the accused admitted taking elvers, but denied that elvers are the fry of eels. In answer to this, the prosecution put Mr Hawkins, a fish-dealer into the stand.

He told the court how he was in the habit of stocking a gentleman's pond at Cheltenham with fish, and at times had put buckets of elvers into these ponds. Afterwards eels had been brought out. He had also stated that he had placed elvers in to glasses, (glass tanks I would suppose), with silver fish, and when he took them out believed them to be small eels. [9]

To bolster the prosecution, Severn Fisheries Board once more dispatched bailiff Huxley, who outlined to the court the elver to eel cycle, based as it was on his years of observation. In the event, he believed the elvers to be the fry of eels. [9]

However, the combined evidence of Hawkins and Huxley, were unable to convince the bench. (Captain De Winton, an ex conservator, appeared unable to exercise any clout on this one). For the first and only time, an elver prosecution case was dismissed, and the men walked free.

A few days later on 30th April 1874 Three men were brought before Whitminster magistrates for the same offence. Keith Palmer booked 2nd April on the Severn, Quedgeley pleaded not guilty. Asked as to whether he was aware of the notices on the riverbank, he stated he could not read or write.

The Fines were as follows: [10]

Keith Palmer   Found guilty 10/- fine or seven days hard labour.
John Smith   Found guilty 10/- fine or seven days hard labour.
William Perkins   Found guilty 10/- fine or seven days hard labour.

They paid up. Whitminster was a severe country court, and took a dim view of poaching cases. No fine points of debate here - Settlement up front, or else!

As the dispute lengthened, Whitminster would be the first to hand out prison sentences.

The Scam

Back at Gloucester however, the Severn Fisheries Board were grappling with the legal niceties thrown up by the verdict of April 25th. What then is an elver? The question had to be answered and soon; because shortly - another batch of elvering lawbreakers were to appear before the bench.

This time the Board did call upon the services of Frank Buckland, to answer the question. Buckland himself was an 'Inspectorate of Her Majesties Fisheries', editor of the magazine 'Land & Water', and a recognized naturalist in his own right. Furthermore, his close association with the Fisheries Boards had seen him personally involved in the formulation of the 1873 Salmon Act itself.

Hopefully Buckland, could by some scientific means, prove conclusively as to whose parentage the elver belonged to. Frank studied the question, and rapidly came to a conclusion. Without question, he could prove that the elver was the progeny of the eel. This is what he came up with.

Using the technique of comparative anatomy, he examined the transparent elver under a microscope, and noted that its heart was located near its tail, - which he observed is precisely where the heart of an adult eel is to be found. This anatomical peculiarity differing from other freshwater fish was presented as conclusive proof that elvers were indeed the brood of eel. [11]

Except of course, the scientific evidence was a load of old Malarkey. Frank Buckland sold a pup, and everybody bought it. In fact this fallacy long endured; passing into Twentieth Century Gloucester folklore and beyond.

As a kid fishing the canal at Hempsted in the Fifties, I was gravely informed by the older boys that an eel's heart was in its tail, and I would not be at all surprised if there are some Gloucester anglers entertaining this very notion today.

ADULT EUROPEAN EEL: *ANGUILLA ANGUILLA*

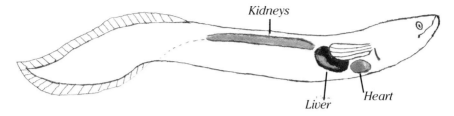

Looking at the front book cover, the position of the elvers heart can be clearly seen just below its head. It can be further observed, that unlike its adult counterpart (see diagram above) no other major organs are present.

Having metamorphosed from the lava 'leptocephalus', it has yet to adjust to freshwater conditions before it starts to feed, and its other organs begin to develop.

At Tewkesbury court, 7th May 1874, James Williams was booked for elvering at Forthampton on 20th April last. He also tried to argue that elvers were not the fry of eel but a different species. The Severn Fisheries Board was ready to counter. Mr H George, Worcester clerk for SFB prosecuted, and bailiff Huxley appeared as witness. They won the case. [12]

James Williams: Fined 1/- and 12/7d costs.

At Newnham Petty Sessions, 16th May 1874, Daniel Smith was caught elvering at Westbury on Severn. Huxley introduced some elvers to court and satisfied the magistrates that they were the fry of eels.

Daniel Smith: Fined 10/- and £1-1s costs. [13]

(Cost inclusion, made this the biggest single fine of the whole dispute).

For the Severn Fisheries Board these were a couple of good results, but the authorities wanted no further slip ups, and nothing was to be left to chance. At the Gloucester court hearings May 23rd 1874, those accused, found themselves confronted by an imposing array of past and present Board officials; both on the bench, and acting for the prosecution.

Magistrates sitting Gloucester 23th May 1874:

Captain Price	Tibberton Court.
Vernon William Guise Baronet	Elmore Court.
Rev J Lysons	Hempsted Court.
E G Halliwell	Beachamps Lodge.
Captain De Winton	Wallsworth Hall.
T Marling	Claremont House.

On this occassion Captain De Winton was in good company. Captain Price and Sir Vernon William Guise were Board members. Both Guise, and Rev J Lysons, owned Severn fisheries at Elmore and Hempsted respectively. [8]

The case for the prosecution was brought by Severn Fisheries Water Inspector, Edmond Escort; and prosecution witnesses included Frank Buckland, and bailiff Huxley.

In the face of this pre-eminent line up, guilty verdicts were all but inevitable. Frank Buckland sealed the accused fate by presenting an elver under a microscope, for the courts inspection. Looking for themselves, the magistrates were able to confirm that they could clearly see the elvers heart beating in its tail. Frank Buckland further asserted that if you wish to kill an eel, it must be "hit on the tail and not the head". [11]

(Mr Francillon again present in court and sitting near Mr Buckland, interjected with abrupt remarks whilst this evidence was given).

The magistrates were now of the opinion that it had been conclusively proven beyond all doubt that the elver was the brood of the eel, and those up before the bench, were guilty as charged.

The Accused: George Price, William Prosser, Joseph Hook, William Martin.

George Price	Fishing 3rd April	Hempsted	Fined 1/-costs 7/-
	Fishing 16th April	Barton St Mary	Fined 1/-costs 7/-
	Fishing 1st May	Hempsted	Fined 1/-costs 7/-

Frank Buckland Photograph: CEFAS Library, Lowestoft Suffolk. NR33 0HT

George Price was a particularly stubborn character summoned three times in just under a month, putting him 24/- out of pocket. (A couple of week's wages I should think). He also used the alias of Bill Tongue, which was one of the names given in the 25th April Court hearings. Seemingly Tongue and Price were one and the same man. [11]

William Prosser fishing 14th April Minsterworth   Fined 1/- costs 11/-
                                                   Including Witness costs 4/-

Jo Hook   fishing 31st March Minsterworth   Fined 1/- costs 11/-
                                                   Including Witness costs 4/-   [8]

William Martin discharged. His name was taken, on 31st March Minsterworth, along with Joe Hook. I guess the net belonged to Joe.

The First Year Ends

For the elvermen, the bank side encounters with the bailiffs seems to have brought forth an honest response when their identity was requested. They were for the most part straightforward blokes.

Attending Gloucester court that same day, five men were charged with the destruction of a public notice board at the Rea, Hempsted. Why it warranted such treatment, court records don't say, but it's obvious what had aroused their ire. It's further safe to surmise that at least one of the accused must have been able to read.

In the event: Thomas Rea, William Ballard, John Boseley, Robert Gibsen and George Hartland, suffered their names and addresses to be taken and were subsequently fined 1/- damages, @ 2/6 costs each. [8]

Things went badly for these men. After all, the vandalizing of one river side notice board would hardly need the collective energies of all five. The bailiffs no doubt aided by the police, concluded that all were guilty by association. Given the widespread hostility toward the elver-ban, these riverbank confrontations (usually taking place at night), could easily have turned nasty, but as yet this had not happened.

In the end, it came down to this. Those who made the laws enforced them, as the elvermen and their supporters now discovered to their cost. Righteous indignation began to bubble up on Gloucester streets, as the ordinary workfolk took stock of the judicial measures being used to prevent their time honoured fishing traditions.

For centuries past the little elver had washed up in lowly obscurity along the springtime Gloucestershire waterways. Now suddenly, and in the space of a few short weeks, it had become the centre of hot dispute between the local landowners, and Gloucester townsfolk.

As the spring of 1874 gave way to summer, the elver season passed, and the prosecution cases dried up. These unfolding events must have privately worried those Gloucester civic dignitaries holding dual office on the Severn Fisheries Board.

As City members, they would be directly accountable to any queries or complaints regarding this whole business. Thirty miles and a county away, Worcester HQ officials were conveniently removed from any prospective hassle the new law brought in its wake.

Still, the Gloucester councillors could take some comfort in the knowledge that many of the elvering fraternity weren't eligible to vote - and it was early days yet. Perhaps the next spring, everything would calm down.

Easy Days

The elver season of 1875, came and went with barely a whimper. There was only case brought at Gloucester that year.

At Gloucester Petty Sessions Shire Hall 17th April 1875:

Joseph Hopkins elvering 6th April Ashleworth Fined 6d   7/6d costs
Solomon Barnes elvering 6th April Ashleworth Fined 6d   7/6d   costs
Henry Pool   elvering 6th April Ashleworth Fined 6d   7/6d   costs [14]

They were allowed a fortnight to pay-quite reasonable too. It seemed that the reality of the ban had sunk in, and compliance now accorded with this changed state of affairs. The Board could congratulate itself.

Doubtless from year to year, one or two mavericks would be periodically brought to book, but Hey! That's why you employ bailiffs. To all intents and purposes the elver could now migrate en-masse through Severn waters, to Worcester and beyond.

Defiance

It was the lull before the storm. The 1876 elver season came in with a bang. Events kicked off on 24th March, with boatloads of Gloucester men, making their way downriver to Epney, presumably in the hope of eluding the bailiffs.

Unfortunately for them, bailiff Huxley was a relentless pursuer of naughty elvermen, and had tracked them all the way. Huxley noted twenty men in boats. They went upriver to Longney Cribb - Huxley followed and thereafter accosted four men: William Worrall, William Manley, Charles Harper and William Powell. They were later charged to appear on 27th April at Whitminster court.

Meantime at Gloucester courts 15th April 1876, ten men were hauled up before magistrates: Sir WV Guise. Thomas De Winton, Thomas Marling and J D Birchall. All were found found guilty of fishing for elvers, between 1st Jan and 29th June.

	Date	Place	Fined	Costs	Default
John Vick	7th April	Elmore	10/-	12/-	7 days hard labour
Richard Cale	7th April	Hempsted	10/-	12/-	7 days hard labour
Henry Cale	7th April	Hempsted	10/-	12/-	7 days hard labour
William Smith	7th April	Ashleworth	10/-	11/6	7 days hard labour
Thomas Jelf	7th April	Maisemore	10/-	11/6	7 days hard labour
Charles Halford	7th April	Maisemore	10/-	11/-	7 days hard labour
John Stephens	7th April	Maisemore	10/-	13/-	7 days hard labour
William Hartland	8th April	Sandhurst	10/-	11/6	7 days hard labour
Henry Wheeldon	8th April	Sandhurst	10/-	11/6	7 days hard labour
Charles Curtis	8th April	Ashleworth	10/-	11/6	7 days hard labour

There was a fortnight to pay

(Note John Vick fished on Land owned by presiding Magistrate, Sir WV Guise).

Yet again Mr Escort trotted out the evidence for the prosecution that elvers were the fry of eels - and again Huxley, (by now quite fed up I should think), along with other police constables presented their findings.

It seemed that the authorities were now having a lively time bringing the elvermen to book, as the lawbreakers, now fully on their toes, had ready made countermeasures of their own.

Forward scouts with dogs had been deployed along Severn banks to stand guard. As soon as the bailiffs/police drew near, the scouts would alert their fishing companions with loud whistles, whereupon the elvermen would bundle their booty and nets into a moored boat, and cast off beyond reach of the law. [16]

From the evidence recorded, these catch or chase shenanigans went on into the early hours of the morning. Some however were not quite so mobile. William Smith at Ashleworth, was booked in possession of an elver net, a bag of elvers, a small basket and a wheelbarrow. [14]

Others when cautioned were defiant. Henry Wheeldon was taken down as saying, "you have got my name, now I'll go on and catch some more to pay my rent". (Wheeldon would go to prison on default of fine). [14]

Pc Etheridge cautioned four men in a boat, with the words, "you'd better be off". One of the men called out, "let's fetch the ----- back, and pitch him in!" Things were turning nasty now. [15]

Above all, the baliffs and police constables repeatedly drew the attention of the bench to the numbers fishing the Severn. At Maisemore, a 'dozen to fourteen men', were noted. Ashleworth had twenty boats counted, whilst at Sandhurst, Huxley reckoned "one hundred and fifty men with boats, nets, and dogs", all out elvering. [14]

After sentences were passed, the bailiffs upon leaving the courthouse had to run the gauntlet of a hooting Gloucester mob.[15]

It was clear enough to all concerned. Full-scale defiance had now become the order of the day. The law-breakers sought to avoid prosecution if they could, but they were going elvering and that was that! This state of affairs could not go on-something had to give, and very swiftly events came to a head.

Imprisonment

On the 27th April, twelve days after the Gloucester prosecutions, Whitminster magistrates: Mr Niblett, Mr Wilton, Mr William Farnham-Clarke and Mr L Darrell presided over what would be a decisive hearing. [10]

The Accused: William Worrall, Vinegar Yard, Gloucester.
William Manley, The Island, (Alney).
Charles Harper, Stephens Yard, Gloucester.
William Powell, Epney. [17]

Charged with elvering at Longney crib on the 24th March 1876.

The prosecution witnesses had caught the accused red handed, (Harper had an elver in a net). Huxley told them to "knock off - they were under the penalty", but defiantly they held their ground. Because of this, and possibly the number of men confronting him, Huxley decided to back off without taking their names. [10]

Next day Huxley returned with P C Owen, and pointed out the culprits, (who had apparently returned to fish the following days tide). There was more defiance and a further refusal to give their names and addresses.

The Whitminster bench must have fairly bristled at the revelation of such goings on. Examples were going to be made; the verdict was handed down - Guilty, and according to the court records:

Worrall was fined 5/- and 14/- Expenses or fourteen days hard labour.
Manley " "   10/- "   15/- Expenses "   "   "   "
Harper " "   10/- "   15/- Expenses "   "   "   "
Powell " "   5/- "   14/- Expenses "   "   "   " [10]

It was immediate payment or prison. Worrall, Manley and Harper unable to pay, found themselves promptly arrested and removed to Gloucester Prison. Powell, who had been tried separately, escaped further attention For the three unfortunates, fourteen days hard labour meant walking the treadmill each day. (The news of these incarcerations, must have 'outraged' Gloucester's west-end.)

The final trial details can be found in Appendix 2.

Impasse

It was the final straw. By May 1876, four men had been imprisoned at Gloucester, - dozens more had been fined, - whilst hundreds were openly defying the law.

Gloucester's body politic now took full alarm at this rebellious state of affairs. The stubborn fight back by the townspeople exposed a fault line between Worcester and Gloucester. The latter civic dignitary's were now anxiously looking to distance themselves from the whole business, lest their tenure of office be jeopardized.

Even with limited voting rights, public opinion still counted, and given the sort of treatment being meted out by the courts, the elvering fraternity had gotten widespread sympathy. For Gloucester's alderman and councillors, It was the town's voters that put them in office, so why risk everything for a bucket of elvers?

With political careers at stake and urged on by all concerned, Gloucester MP's moved quickly to put out the fire. By May 27th it was reported that an 'Elver Fishing Bill' amendment had been brought to the House Of Commons by Mr. Monk (Liberal MP for Gloucester), and Captain Price of Tibberton Court for its first reading. Initially the bill sought simply to repeal that part of section 15 prohibiting the capture of elvers. [18]

Other Gloucester conservators, notably Sir William Vernon Guise and the Rev Lysons, sent letters to the newspaper columns advising Willis-Bund to recognize this "hasty and ill conceived legislation". The schism between Worcester and Gloucester was widening. [18 19]

A further telegram sent from Mr. Wait (Conservative MP for Gloucester), informed the local press that - 'It was the intention of the Government to send one or more inspectors to hold a local inquiry into the case of elver takers, and to report the result of their investigations to the Home Office'. [18]

(In those days two Gloucester MPs were elected to Parliament. On the occasion of the dispute the MP's were Mr Monk and Mr Wait).

Step Forward Commander Francillon

If there was to be an Inquiry however, the pro elver lobby would require somebody to champion their cause. Now it was time for John George Francillon to officially throw his hat into the ring.

Francillon had been prominent in his opposition to the elver ban from the outset, as his earlier court attendances can testify. Untainted by any connection with the Severn Fisheries Board, his political prominence in Gloucester Liberal circles made him the ideal candidate for the job.

Francillon himself was a long standing and respected resident of Gloucester, and in the year 1876, a mere eighty one years young. He was descended from a distinguished family line of seafaring traditions, and at thirteen years of age in 1806 he was placed in the service of the Royal Navy.

He'd sailed on the old timbered warships including the HMS Victory, and served through the Napoleonic wars, and the American wars of 1812-14, until finally aged twenty four, he left the service with the rank of lieutenant. He was ever afterwards addressed by the title of Commander.
Appendix 1

The bulk of his working life was spent at Gloucester docks, where he acted as a Lloyd's shipping agent. Latterly, he himself had forged business interests in the Docks, and owned a passenger boat service, plying the Glos/Sharpness canal.

Above all the man in his younger days was a political activist, who took great pride in his past role agitating for the right of 'the vote' earlier that century. These activists were known as 'radical reformers'. In those days England was a tremble, and on more than one occasion came close to the brink. [4]

By 1876, turbulent England had long since stabilized and industrialized. A 'worthy cause' was now the Liberal catchword, and Francillon had a very unusual one on his hands. In the event, the old campaigner left us a written echo of a passion that had its roots in an earlier campaigning epoch. Public support was the key, and one of his many letters on the elver question appeared in the Gloucester Journal 29th April 1876 - It began:

"Dear Sir-On Saturday the 13th* of this month, *eleven men were mulcted in the sum of twenty-one shillings at the petty sessional court held at the Shire Hall Gloucester. I would most respectfully ask what crime these men have committed?"

(*A Glos Journal error, the court case was 15th April, the accused 10)

He attended the court hearings of 15th April 1876, where the scale of illegal fishing had been revealed, and in his letter, drew attention as to the correctness of the proceedings. Apparently Sir William Vernon Guise had arrived late without hearing all the evidence - yet still found against the elvermen.

Furthermore; according to Francillon elvering did a service toward the preservation of the salmon. It seemed that eels ate samlets, (young salmon), but salmon derived no benefits from the presence of eels, or their young.

(Frank Buckland stated at an earlier court hearing, that the elver was a necessary food source for salmon returning to sea after spawning). [11]

Francillon cited evidence from fishmongers, who stated that in all their years preparing salmon, not one elver had ever been discovered in the digestive systems of that fish. However; the opposite was true when it came to the appetites of eels.

Then of course there was the cost to the ratepayers. The reader's attention was drawn to police resources being diverted to the riverbank, when they could be more properly employed, in their 'proper duties' protecting society.

The more respectable and parsimonious elements of Gloucester society must have been left frowning over their Journals - this wasn't what they paid their district rates for.

Having skillfully presented the case, Francillon now prepared for the showdown. Judicial wheels had turned, and in the following month of June 1876, the awaited general Inquiry was to be held at Gloucester Shire Hall, to examine the elver question.

In the time available to him, Francillon set out on a recruitment drive to mobilize his own supporters, and in pursuance of such ends, he was to turn up in the most unlikely of places.

The White Swan Gloucester: Reproduced by permission of English Heritage. NMR

Rally At The White Swan.

On the Friday night of 19th May 1876, and just three weeks after the Citizen first went to press; a reporter was sent to cover an extraordinary meeting at the White Swan Westgate Street Gloucester. The meeting was convened by those parties opposed to section 15 of the 1873 Salmon Fisheries Act.

The distance between Gloucester Shire Hall and the White Swan was small enough. Both stood on Westgate Street, and a five minute walk was all that separated them; but within these institutions lay two different worlds.

The first was an imposing municipal building, wherein lay high civic office with financial resources at its disposal. The second was a mean watering hole, where the working classes quenched their thirsts at the end of a long working day.

It was the latter venue that saw Commander Francillon lead his team of councillors and interested parties that Friday evening into these spit and sawdust surroundings. According to the reporter, "the room was crowded with fishermen and labourers, enthusiastically gathered" to hear the word.

Councillor Duthbridge (West Ward) was voted into the chair, and doubtless with an eye on the reporter made it clear that he himself had always opposed the elver ban. Then without further ado the first speaker was called upon to address the meeting. Francillon himself rose, whereupon the citizen reporter noted he was greeted with "vociferous applause".

Francillon began his speech by informing the audience that a bill had recently been introduced in the House of Commons by Mr. Monk MP, and its passage was to be aided by another local MP and colleague, Mr. Wait.

The bill would revoke section 15 of the 1873 Act, and allow for elver fishing to legally take place between March 1st and April 30th. This intelligence brought forth further applause from the gathering.

Francillon further drew their attention to a man called *Warren, who had been taken from his family and sent to prison. He was likened to a "martyr", who suffered before "obnoxious laws" in order to get them changed, and that he had "not suffered in vain".

(*This is a mistranslation. The person referred to is Henry Wheeldon, booked at Gloucester court 15th April 1876).

Warming to his speech, and with no small sarcasm, Francillon recounted to the audience, as to a recent exchange of letters between himself and Sir William Vernon Guise. The speaker remarked that Sir William's first letter:

"Deserved to be written in letters of gold, but that the second could only be explained upon the supposition that Sir William had been unable through the multiplicity of his duties to study the question".

"The law at present allowed the public to buy elvers, but prevented fishermen from catching them, however Sir William proposed that it should be legal to catch them, but illegal to eat them!" (Laughter). The inference was clear to all assembled - Sir William was nice but dim.

That Francillon could publicly lambaste a Peer of the Realm in a downtown Gloucester pub to a bunch of labourers was ground breaking stuff, and showed how much times had changed. It was not always so.

Earlier that century, William Fitzhardinge Berkeley took exception to an article written about him in the Cheltenham Journal, and with a few cronies including Lord Sussex Lennox; located the whereabouts of the editor and horsewhipped him. Now up against a rebellious industrial workforce, the landowners involved, were in no position to hand out thrashings. [21]

Francillon himself, was an up 'through the ranks' man, and clearly resented the hereditary peerage system, (in those days a sentiment widely held by the emerging business classes). He would have certainly remembered how the Lords blocked the Commons *enfranchisement bills, back in the 1830's and lost no opportunity to take a swipe in that direction.

*(a bill to extend voting rights)

He had waited "fifty five years for the ballot, and ultimately they had attained it". He believed they would "speedily obtain what he had earnestly desired for the past two years, and that this obnoxious law will be abolished".

To the gathered assembly, Francillon's impressive vocabulary was something they didn't come across too often-especially in the White Swan, but they got the message all the same. The reporter noted, "prolonged cheering", and a voice called out. "Well done Mr Francillon!"

Now the Commander was cruising. He did not dispute that elvers were the fry of eels, but "If all elvers grew into eels" he declared, "the Severn would not be navigable". I imagine the audience went over the moon hearing that one.

He further alluded to the catches of eels behind the Colin Campbell citing the tonnage caught as "showing no sign of scarcity". Interestingly a European dimension was brought to the occasion, as French catches of elver in the Loire was briefly mentioned.

Afterwards a vote of thanks to Messrs Monk and Wait for their assistance was adopted, whereupon the reporter was moved to write. "At this stage Mr Francillon retired to the sound of deafening cheers!"

And that wasn't the end of it by a long chalk. Further speeches by Messrs Sherwood, T Cook, and Worrall, (no doubt recounting his time on the prison mill), held the attention of the audience.

Then, a memorial to the Secretary Of State for the Home Department asking for his support of Mr Monk's bill was adopted. The reporter described the proceedings as "exceedingly animated, concluded shortly before ten".

There was a hot time in the old White Swan that night. High politics were talked; local dignitaries rubbed shoulders with the common crew. In the history of that pub, nothing before could have stood comparison. Now the troops were rallied, all was in readiness and expectations were sky high. - I wish I'd been there.

The Gloucester Inquiry [4]

And so on the 8th June 1876, at a time when Britannia ruled the waves and held dominion over the largest empire ever seen. The dignitaries and political officials of Gloucester and surrounding districts formally convened at the Old Shire Hall, Westgate Street, Gloucester, in order to gauge the well being of the little elver. It was an inquiry without parallel, and is recorded in the Gloucester Journal.

The proceedings were opened by Her Majesty's Inspectors of Fisheries: Mr *Spencer Walpole and Mr Frank Buckland, acting on the instructions of Mr Cross: Secretary of State for the Home Department.

(Son of Spencer Horatio Walpole, Conservative MP and Home Sec)

The formal position of the enquiry investigation was to look into the operation of the 15th section of the Salmon Fisheries Act 1873 by which it is enacted that, 'no person between the 1st day of Jan and 24th June inclusive, shall hang fix or use in any salmon river, any baskets nets traps or devices for catching eels, or the fry of eels'.

The impressive turnout that day saw Commander J G Francillon assisted by *Mr H Y J Taylor appearing on behalf of the elver fishers in support of an alteration to the law.

(Henry Yates Jones Taylor, or HYJT as he initialed himself, worked as a clerk in Gloucester Docks. He was a local historian and sometime poet).

Mr J W Willis-Bund represented himself on behalf of the Severn Fisheries Board. Also present was Captain Price and Mr Boxall - a Government lawyer; The Rev Cannon Lysons, Mr G Riddiford, Mr W V Ellis and other conservators also attended.

It was clear that before the actual Inquiry, a certain amount of horse - trading had taken place, and the opposing parties had reached a tentative outline of an elvering close season. In his opening remarks to the gathered assembly, Mr Willis-Bund admitted "a certain revision in the law was desirable", and both sides agreed 1st March as season start.
4

The problem lay in when the elvering season was to close. Willis-Bund proposed the 20th April as the final day of the season. Francillon insisted that the season last ten more days until 30th April.

Roughly speaking there are two high tides in a month, and usually by the 20th April the second cycle of high tides has peaked. On the face of it Willis-Bunds proposal to set the end of season at this date seemed reasonable enough. Traditional elvering after all takes place in March & April.

However it's not quite as neat as that. The tidal cycle is constantly shifting across the calendar, and sometimes the spring high tides are later, with the April second tide rising at the end of that month. The extension to the 30th would enable these tides to be fished.

The close season argument set aside for the time being, the main thrust of the enquiry began. The protagonists Francillon and Willis-Bund, were now free to call any relevant witnesses in pursuance of their case.

As we have already seen Francillon himself placed great reliance on the evidence of the ordinary river people caught up in this dispute, and consequently a wonderful procession of Victorian characters took the stand to give evidence. Their views, theories and conditions of life recorded and preserved forever, thanks to this remarkable enquiry.

The first man called was George James, an elderly man from Elmore who had been taking elvers for fifty years and had never been interfered with until the last two years. He sold them at 1-1/2 to 2d a pound and people had told him there was "more stay in them than beef". The elvers were sold on to people in Elmore and Gloucester. His father had brought up twelve children with the help of elver fishing, and he had done the same.

He told the enquiry that the best bait for eels was a bib of salmon, and that eels eat eels. He made his second point by way of a story wherein his son had caught two on one line, (a night line I would guess). The first had swallowed the hook; the second had swallowed the first. [4]

He had seen two hundred men out fishing, and that in his opinion the only persons benefiting from the elver ban were the "bum bailiffs" who would have to distrain for rent.

(As far as I can understand from that remark, it would seem that without money from elver fishing, the rent could not be paid heralding the arrival of the bum baliffs to remove possessions in lieu of payment).

In answer to Mr Willis-Bund as to how close he lived by the river, he remarked that sometimes he lived in the river, because very often the river came into his house. (laughter)

H J Y T. told the enquiry that he had weighed an ounce of elvers and found there were 90, making 1,440 to the pound. He also referred to autumnal netting of eels at the back of the docks, where he had heard that on one occasion five tons of eels were caught in one night-as a result he not think eels had diminished lately.

George Spiers also from Elmore had been fishing for fifty two years and interviewed by Mr Francillon said he had taken 2cwt in a night, and that he considered elver fishing of great benefit to the poor man. He believed eels destructive of salmon spawn, for they would eat anything they could catch hold of.

When questioned by Mr Buckland, he said that years ago he used to feed elvers to his pigs - and that there were as many elvers running up the river as when he was a young man. He always sold his elvers at home and that he had noticed a difference in elvers. Some had sharper noses than others.

As the inquiry progressed, and more witnesses were called to the stand, over and again, those questioned, stressed the benefit of the elver to the poor, and that the ban had caused much hardship. In order to press home his point, Francillon called those very men who had been jailed.

The Prisoner's Plight

All four men imprisoned were corn porters employed at Gloucester docks. Their task was to shovel out the grain from the holds of the incoming boats; bag up the grain and barrow the bags to the warehouses.

At the time of the elver runs, the corn porters were seasonally laid off, and therefore by time honoured tradition, had turned to the elver harvest for income and food.

So the ban had hit these unemployed men hard, and explains the lengths they had gone to, in order to keep fishing. Longney Cribb is some way down river from Gloucester, and consequently brought them under the jurisdiction of Whitminster courts.

From Gloucester cross to Whitmister is a good eight miles. Worrall, Manley and Harper must have walked penniless to the courthouse, and in default of fine were immediately placed in cuffs, and escorted on foot back to Gloucester prison.

Francillon, by drawing attention to this state of affairs, caused the inquiry great embarrassment. Mr Walpole conceded that the magistrates had overstepped their mark, and did not have the power to jail a man without a previous conviction-nor had the accused been given time to distrain. *(Pay the fine)*

At this point Mr Francillon became angry, describing the treatment of these men as "monstrous!", and shortly engaged Mr Willis-Bund, Mr Walpole and Mr Buckland with indignant retorts. The latter parties attempted to placate his outburst, with reassurances that the evidence presented thus far, be included in the inquiry.

The forth man to be jailed was yet another unemployed corn porter named in the Gloucester Journal as 'Albert Wildon'.

(This is Henry Wheeldon again, and once more his name has been mistakenly transcribed. He is almost certainly the man called Warren at the meeting in the White Swan. This particular surname gave the recorders no end of trouble).

He had seven days to pay his fine, but on default the police came at 11 pm, roused him from his bed and removed him to prison to serve seven days hard labour. Pressed by Willis-Bund, Wheeldon had no recollection of Francillon calling out in the court room. "Go to prison men, and be martyrs!"

It sounds to me the sort of thing he would say, but the convicted men paid their fines. Wheelden obviously flat broke, simply carried on regardless until overtaken by events.

The Interrogation

Now it was the turn of Willis-Bund to be cross-examined by Francillon. From the outset Francillon was determined to get to the bottom of Willis-Bund's part in the introduction of section 15. He had after all, been a key adviser to the select committee formulating the 1873 Salmon Fisheries Act.

Francillon was convinced that Willis-Bund had personally overseen the insertion of the crucial sentence 'the fry of eels', and closely interrogated the witness, in order to gain an admission.

Initially Willis-Bund would not be drawn and declined to answer, but in response to persistent questioning, denied any personal responsibility as to the inclusion of the vexatious words.

Whist on the stand Willis-Bund made some observations regarding elver and eel returns above Gloucester. He stated that in the upper waters of late years, eels and elver catches had fallen off, but since the ban it was noticed that the quantities of eels (spared elvers) had increased.

He did not attribute the falling off of elvers prior to the 1873 Act as the result of the weirs built at Gloucester and Tewkesbury, but that the diminutions in the upper came from those caught lower down.

However, prior evidence seemed to contradict Willis-Bunds assertion. Charles Aston, an elver man for more than thirty years used to catch plenty of elvers above Tewkesbury but now Tewkesbury weir stopped them. He had seen dead balls of elvers below Tewkesbury, and Maisemore weirs.

Those Five Little Words

The second day, 9th June, Willis-Bund again took the stand, and described in great detail how the legislation in question came to pass. In the process of which, he went no small way to substantiate Francillon's suspicions of'or his direct authorship in the matter.

The birth of 'or the fry of eel' inclusion into section 15 was quite remarkable. The authorities in their search for a suitable statute had to dig deep into the annals of past game laws.

Unfortunately for them, the Act of Charles 11 1667 outlawing elver fishing, was repealed by the Act of George 111 1778, restoring fishing rights to those living in close proximity to the Severn and Vrynwy, for personal consumption only.

Therefore it was the Act of Elizabeth 1 1558 which they finally plumped for. The crucial words forbade fishing, 'for the preservation of spawn, and the fry of fish'. The only query that remained, was whether the eel qualified as a fish?

When it finally was established to the satisfaction of the select committee that the eel was undoubtedly a fish, the 1558 statute was dusted down, and three hundred and fifteen years later, inserted into section 15 of the 1873 Act.

Furthermore just to ensure there was no confusion, the entry 'or the fry of eels' was added, the reason being is that it did not amend the Act of Elizabeth 1, but made the law clearer, where eels and elvers were concerned.

The Worcester Inquiry [22]

All in all, the entire inquiry lasted three days. Thursday 8th June and Friday 9th June were conducted at Gloucester Shire Hall, whilst the final day Saturday 10th June was convened at Worcester. Now it was the turn of J W Willis-Bund, to present the other point of view.

Unlike the ordinary river men called to testify by Commander Francillon, much of the evidence came from the Worcester based conservators, and their employees.

The dearth of elvers above Tewkesbury was given much prominence. This was clearly a river of two halves- the uppers were the eel, and the downers were elver.

Baliff Huxley gave evidence on behalf of the Severn Fisheries Board. He remembered as a boy at Bewdley, seeing elvers caught by children, scooping them out of the water using sieves.

Other witnesses, among them the Major of Worcester recalled similar scenes taking place at Worcester thirty-seven years earlier. He described the elvers as "lining the sides of the river banks", and children catching them using baskets and colanders.

"Shoals" comparable to Gloucester was the expression used by other witnesses to describe their past appearances. Now at the time of the inquiry these "shoals" of elver had fallen away.

A further claim as to the past abundance of elvers up river was given in evidence by a Mr F Allen, described in the Gloucester Journal as "from a long acquaintance with fishing matters".

He testified that elvers ran up the Teme as high as Bransford, two miles above Powick weir in his early days. "Almost every fish-kelts, chubb, trout - fed on them when they were running. An elver was a very killing bait for them".

Francillon, in his cross examination of the witnesses, gained admissions from them that when tides were high, the Tewkesbury weir was breached and elvers still came over.

He further drew attention to the fact that the diminution of eel catches up river, might be explained by the large increase of eel traps and nets over the past twenty years; and that the same amount of eels running down in the autumn were having to be shared by more interested parties.

At the end of the third day, after the final summing up speeches by Mr J W Willis-Bund and Commander J G Francillon, both Mr Walpole and Mr Buckland, of 'Her Majesty's Inspectors of Fisheries', assured the opposing parties that they would, "honestly and fairly consider the interests of the parties concerned". Shortly afterwards Mr Walpole declared the inquiry closed.

It was now down to these inspectors to write their report on the inquiry proceedings, and after examining the evidence, present their recommendations as to how the elver question was to be resolved.

With Mr Monks Elver bill, already making progress through Parliament, the report was essentially viewed by all concerned as a touchstone. Any salient points and relevant observations made by the report, stood to become incorporated into the bill itself.

At this time of course, nobody was sure what the reports recommendations might be, and some points would inevitably be contested by the opposing parties.

The bill's original intent to strike out the offending words relating to the fry of eel had been rejected by the Willis-Bund camp. They wanted conditions attached to the lifting of the ban. Sympathetic Worcestershire MP's stood by in readiness to deliver parliamentary support for this position if necessary. The dispute was far from over.

The Report

On Sat June 24th 1876, the Gloucester Journal printed the findings of Her Majesty's Inspectorate, Mr Spencer Walpole and Mr Frank Buckland. Coincidentally Mr Monk's bill was to be presented to Parliament that same day. The report took precedence, and the bill deferred.

As it stood the report recommended immediately lifting a ban on elver fishing on all other rivers except the Severn, which was a bit strange because on no other waterway but the Severn, was the ban ever enforced in the first place.

Indeed, Usk conservators were on record as being 'most desirous to see the ban lifted, as a continuation of this law would compel them to enforce it, which they would be most reluctant to comply with'.

So in contrast to the rest of the countries waterways, the Severn uniquely was to have a close elvering season - and this time the sale of elvers were to be included in the amendment.

The 1873 Act, whilst it prohibited the catching of elvers had unfortunately omitted to include their sale. This embarrassing oversight meant that those able evade the bailiffs and get off the bank side with their booty, could freely and openly trade in the usual customary fashion.

The defiant rows of chairs and basins set out on Gloucester streets boldly advertising their wares, (perhaps sometimes only yards from the Severn itself), made a mockery of the whole business.

It was this issue which had prompted an 11th hour intervention by Mr Willis-Bund applying to the Home Secretary to re-open the enquiry, but by now the application would not be entertained.

However the parliamentary horse trading went on, and the Willis-Bund camp conditionally prepared to withdraw opposition to Mr Monk's bill, if a clause was inserted banning the sale of Severn elvers out of season.

The report dutifully concluded with a personal reservation made by Mr Frank Buckland, stating, that the Inspectorate would only go as far as to recommend the legalizing of Severn elver fishing conditional on a close season, but it was his personal view that during these closed times the "sale" of elvers from the Severn must also be prohibited as well.

As to the when the elver fishing season should be, 1st March had been agreed by the disputing parties to be the start date, but the sticking point came as to season end. The pro elver camp, wanted 30th April, but the Severn Fisheries Board the 20th.

The report suggested a compromise by splitting the difference. The season 1st March to 25th April was put forward as an alternative, and this eventually became the accepted times when Severn elver could be taken and sold.

At the time of the report, belief was widespread, that more than one species of eel resided in Britain's inland waterways. The Inspectorate was no exception, and the report went so far as to identify three species: The broad nosed eel, the sharp-nosed eel, and the snig eel.

Locally, a first year elver was known as a 'stick eel', the following year a 'shuntling', and the third year an 'eel'. I remember as kids we called all small eels 'bootlaces'.

The inspectorate also gave consideration to the desirability of licensed elvering, as earlier that month during the enquiry Mr Willis-Bund had suggested the introduction of a yearly elver licence at 2/- per net.

In the end however, the Inspectorate rejected this proposal citing the fact that shrimp, twait and eel nets paid no licence duty. As a result the report did not think it advisable to proceed further in this direction. Which was rather a shame, as this information would have thrown light on the extent of elvering activity at that time?

The Terms

And so the report and its recommendations were presented before Parliament in June 1876, but Mr Monk's bill did not receive Royal Assent until late in July. The clause sought by Mr Willis-Bund as to the sale of elvers out of season proved troublesome, and amendments had to be added to the satisfaction of Worcester MP Mr Hill, before the bill could proceed. [23]

In the event, the clause listed Gloucestershire's parish hundreds, where catching and selling of elvers became illegal during the close season. The hundreds so named were: Kiftegate, Deerhurst, Dudstone, Kings Barton, Berkeley, Westminster, Dutchy of Lancaster, Westbury and Tewkesbury.

(Curiously the Whitstone hundreds were omitted, thereby exempting the Severn parishes of Frampton on Severn, Fretherne, Longney, Saul, Moreton Valance and Whitminster from the clause forbidding sale).

Thereafter; anybody found fishing for-or trading elvers in the listed hundreds between April 26th and the last day of February, would be liable to a fine not exceeding 20s, unless they could prove the elvers were not Severn caught.

So how can you tell an elver is from the Wye, and not the Severn? The Gloucester Journal noted these inconsistencies but concluded, "It was deemed best to accept this absurd amendment, rather than lose the bill which may now be considered as passed through all its perils having been set down for final consideration on Thursday night". [23]

Finally, to the great relief of both civic dignitaries and elvermen alike, the 29th July 1876 edition of The Gloucester Journal briefly noted, "the elver bill received royal assent by commission on Monday". Mr Monk's bill-warts and all, was passed 24th July 1876, allowing seasonal elver fishing to resume on the Severn.

The breaking news was displayed on posters outside Citizen offices, and all concerned in the struggle to lift the ban could congratulate themselves on a job well done. After three years of strife, Gloucester folk had won back their time honoured birthright.

Frayed Tempers

The whole business that summer of 1876, called forth a partisan approach between the uppers of Worcester, and downers, of Gloucester. The war of words rolled back and forth along the Severn between the two Cities respective newspapers- each backing their home crowd.

The Gloucester Journal gave fulsome praise to Commander Francillon's defence of the Gloucester elvermen, and were duly critical of Mr Willis-Bund. At one point they hinted at his personal fisheries interest as the motivating factor behind the ban. (Mr Willis-Bunds estates at Worcester Episcopi bounded both the Severn and Teme, wherein fisheries were rented). [24]

Equally dutiful, the Worcester Herald lined up with the Worcester conservators, and defended the fishing ban as an entirely proper attempt to save the eel population from the Gloucester elvermen, and with it the livelihoods of the eel men further up river. [25]

At one point in the July 1st 1876 edition of the Gloucester Journal, the editor was moved to print a warning notice above the 'Letters to the Editor' column stating that: - "We cannot open our columns, to complaints of other papers".

On the same page, H Y J T, writing a letter headed "Eel Passes", patronizingly invited Worcester to take note of the enlightened eel fisheries on the river Bann in Ireland.

According to HYJT, these fisheries installed eel passes unlike Worcester. He sarcastically concluded, "I think our Worcester friends may learn an important lesson from the eel fisheries of the Bann. Paddy is evidently in advance of the wise men of Worcester and Salop".

For his part Willis-Bund attending a meeting of the 'Fisheries Preservation Association', announced that the elver bill before Parliament, "sanctioned the destruction of what constituted a large portion of food for the lower classes". [26]

'The Field' magazine also waded in and adding fuel to the fire vehemently criticized the handling of the inquiry, especially (and here the finger was pointed at Commander Francillon), the taking of evidence from ordinary elverman.

'The Field' lamented that throughout proceedings no eminent naturalists or Ichthyologists were called to the stand. As far as they were concerned this was a complete waste of time and public money, and they said so too.

"Why" (they asked), "it should be thought necessary to take evidence from various ignorant prejudiced fishermen who were anxious to be allowed to destroy the eel fishery of the Severn, we could not imagine!"

Furthermore, in order to press home their point as to the undesirability of these low types on the witness stand, they added. "And if evidence were required that congers become porpoises at the full of the moon, somebody might be found who would be quite prepared to come forward and swear to it!- and very likely if his credulity were properly fed and excited, actually to believe it too!" [26]

As the summer wore on, the heated exchanges gave way, to a more sedate correspondence. For those who chose to dwell on the subject, it was now simply a matter of picking over the pieces, which they did.

Somebody it seems had found an old timer residing in a workhouse, who recalled a similar occasion passed down orally to him by his father or grandfather, when previous elver restrictions passed by George 111 Act had also found local champions prepared to go and see George 111 and fight for the poor mans elvering rights. [27]

In the event nobody could find any written proof of such a claim, and slowly that summer all that could be said about the business was said. The correspondence concerning the little elver began to fade from the newspaper columns, and the dispute passed into history.

Aftermath

Elvering could once more commence along the Severn, but now with a close season. For Gloucester elvermen this meant little or nothing. The previous ban had proved to be absolutely unworkable, so enforcing a close season would fare no better, and as far as I can tell, no further prosecutions were ever brought before court. Anyway it didn't matter, because when it suited them - the fishermen had a trump card to play.

Occasionally when the season had been poor, such as brought on by excess flood water, or a late winter thaw, a Gloucester delegation of elvermen would petition Gloucester Board Officials, and respectfully request for an extension to the season. [28]

The petition was duly delivered to Worcester Head Offices for inspection. Protocol thus observed, permission for an extension to fish was unfailingly granted. This state of affairs went on for sixty years until 1935 when the 1876 amendment, was finally repealed, and once more elver fishing on the Severn could be freely entered into. [2e]

So was there any justification for the ban in the first place? Whatever the situation then, there is no doubt that the warnings given were prophetic, as we do now have a real crisis regarding the future of the elver/eel.

From the articles and statements at the time, there seemed to be a great abundance of elvers. Indeed veteran elvermen today would take the view that the decline in elver catches only came to pass within the last thirty years or so. Perhaps however, the dispute was a harbinger of the first signs of failing elver numbers.

Cluster Theory

The overall elver population in Britain was never in question. The complete lack of action to ban elver fishing on any other waterways but the Severn is proof plenty of the narrow three counties view that prevailed within the Worcester offices of the Severn Fisheries Board.

A view which in all fairness derived from a complete ignorance of the eel's reproductive cycle, as Frank Buckland's evidence given to Gloucester court in 1874 demonstrated at the time.

He believed that eels ran down to the estuary in autumn, where the spawn was deposited in the mud. The following spring, the eggs hatched into tiny elvers and made their way back inland. [11]

It follows from such thinking that Severnside eels brought forth Severnside elvers on a seasonal basis, and was therefore a self sustaining population, whose breeding range extended to the Bristol Channel only.

Willis-Bund gave voice to these anxieties at the Inquiry, by calling witnesses to cite the past range of the elver phenomena. Huxley's testimony had them arriving on masse at Bewdley, which is fifty miles above Gloucester.

There is another piece of evidence that suggests an even more remarkable inland elver culture. A century earlier, the 1778 Act of George 111 Chap 33 allowed the taking of elvers from the Severn and Vyrnwy for consumption, but not sale.

The inclusion of the Vyrnwy in this Act is quite startling, especially given its location. This thirty five mile river bordering Wales and Shropshire makes its confluence with the Severn, some one hundred and twenty miles above Gloucester.

Its hard to believe that elvering took place so far up, but why would the legislation include the Vyrnwy, if it was not so?

By 1876, a hundred years later, Tewkesbury was recognised as the high point on the Severn where elvering could be practically undertaken, a fall back from the Vyrnwy of some hundred miles.

At the time of the Gloucester dispute, the pro elver fishing parties presented counter arguments explaining the disappearance of these up river elver spectacles, by citing the imposition of weir and lock emplacements at Upper Lode Tewkesbury and above. *(By this time, there were four weirs between Worcester and Bewdley).*

If you include the canal basins opening into the lower Severn, then migrating elvers were to some measure, dispersed into these artificial waterways, whilst the Severn side shoals became fragmented by the man made obstacles encountered along further upriver.

As a result, the once traditional en masse elver arrivals beyond the tidal influence of the bore, became a piecemeal process, and their discernable impact was lost. Importantly, the elver still reached these higher locations, but not in the same observable manner.

Elvers were taken at Gloucester of course, but not to the extent of threatening the eel populations in any stretch of the waterways under the control of the Severn Fisheries Board. In short; the pro-elver fishing parties argued that there were plenty of elvers/eels to go round.

These arguments look good, and would certainly be hard to discredit, but it may just be that the dispute unintentionally picked up on the wider issue of an overall decline in elver numbers.

It's a long shot but elver clusters noted on other riverside towns or villages in past times could possibly be used as a barometer to gauge whose arguments stood up.

If the elver at one time was being fished as far up as the Vyrnwy, then surely other associated waterways must have been similarly affected. From eyewitness testimony given in the early decades of nineteenth century, the little beast arrived in British waterways in enormous numbers.

Elver Cluster

Glos Journal July 8th 1876. Letter from HYJT, includes information taken from British Cyclopedia Of Natural History by C Partington published 1835: 'Elvers passing along the River Dee Aberdeenshire in lines on either side of the river at not less than four miles an hour for eight days and nights together'.

If such scenes were being witnessed on the Dee, then the Severn, (ere long the elver centre of Britain), must once have heaved with vast springtime shoals. With this in mind, it might be possible to locate the bench mark of elver culture along other waterways within the Severn catchments area.

To put the 'cluster theory' to the test, we have to look below Gloucester, and locate a river largely untouched by weirs and canal locking systems. The Wye seems to fit the bill here. Even today it's mostly rural, and unlike the Severn, never became a major shipping river. At the moment elvering survives at Llandogo, and Brockweir, in the Wye valley.

If later 19th Century elver numbers bore comparison to earlier eyewitness descriptions, then at the time of the 1876 enquiry, it's not unreasonable to expect elver capture taking place further along the Wye itself.

The market towns of Monmouth or Ross on Wye spring to mind as a possible source of past elver fishing culture. Perhaps even Hereford might have something to tell us. If elvering at these locations could be verified at this time - the pro-elver fishing position would seem to be correct, and elver numbers were holding up.

However; If the opposite was found, and at the time of the dispute elver capture remained traceable only to the same locations as exist today, then this suggests a fall back was taking place throughout the 19th Century, and history's verdict would favour the Severn Fisheries Board.

One way or the other, the hard part will be locating any documentary information that can help us resolve the matter. After all, to the ordinary riverside villagers and townspeople of olden days, the once commonplace arrival of the little elver, would excite no more comment than the coming of the swallows- and bit by bit, all becomes lost to memory - Sadly.

Gloucester Records Office:

1. 1871 Gloucester prison census.
2. (a) (b) (c) (d) (e) Fishing on the lower Severn: John Neuvfille Taylor
3. Elver fishing on the river Severn: John Neufville Taylor MR1.22GS
4. Gloucester Journal: June10th 1876
5. Severn Fisheries Board: D1047
6. Tewkesbury Register: SATURDAY APRIL 4TH 1874
7. Gloucestershire Census Returns: ROL. H14
8. Gloucester Petty Session Court Records: PS/GL M1/6
9. Gloucestershire Chronicle: MAY 2ND 1874
10. Whitminster Petty Sessions Court: PS/WH M1/3
11. Gloucester Chronicle: MAY 30th 1874
12. Tewkesbury Register: SATURDAY MAY 9th 1874
13. Tewkesbury Register: SATURDAY MAY 16th 1874
14. Gloucester Petty Session Court Records: PS/GL/M1/7
15. Gloucester Chronicle: APRIL 22nd 1876
16. Gloucester Standard: APRIL 22nd 1876
17. Gloucester Chronicle: APRIL 29th1876
18. Gloucester Chronicle: MAY 27th 1876
19. Gloucester Chronicle: MAY 6th 1876
20. Appendix 1
21. Gloucester Journal: March 21st 1825
22. Gloucester Journal: June 17th 1876
23. Gloucester Journal: July 8th 1876
24. Gloucester Journal: June10th1876
25. Gloucester Chronicle: June 3rd1876
26. Gloucester Journal: July 1st 1876
27: Gloucester Journal: July 29th 1876
28: Gloucester Journal: April 30th 1910

Worcester Records Office:

John William Willis-Bund Portrait: Ref 899 701 BA 8415
Severn Fisheries Board Map: File No 899:113 Book Ref 11,431

Other:

Frank Buckland Photograph: CEFAS Library, Lowestoft Suffolk. NR33 0HT
The White Swan Gloucester: Reproduced by permission of English Heritage. NMR

Appendix 1:
John George Francillon Obituary, Gloucester Journal July 9th 1881

DEATH OF MR. J. G. FRANCILLON.—We regret to announce the death of this gentleman, which took place at his residence, Sudbrook, on Thursday night. Deceased belonged to a French Protestant family, which sought refuge in this country in 1684, in consequence of the revocation of the Edict of Nantes. He was born in 1794, and was consequently 87 years years of age when he died. He was the third son of Captain Francis Francillon, R.N., and was born at Harwick. He entered the navy in 1807, as a boy of the 2nd class on board the "Pompee," and was consequently transferred to the "Victory," being on service in the North Sea. In 1808 he became a volunteer of the 1st class on board the "Pompee," with the Channel fleet, and was present at the capture of the "Martinique." Afterwards, in 1809, he became a midshipman on board the "Belleisle," and saw service in the West Indies, and in the Channel in 1811. The same and following year he was present at the siege of Cadiz in the "Implacable," and "Alfred." In March, 1812, he was a midshipman on board the "Ganymede," and sailed from Cadiz to England to join Sir George Cockburn in the "Grampus." In 1813, he was a midshipman on the "Malabar," on boat service at Cadiz, and on the coast of America; and was transferred in a similar capacity to the "Sceptre" in 1814, being placed in command of a tender. He afterwards joined the "Albion." He passed as lieutenant on December 14th, 1818, and subsequently left the navy. Mr. Francillon was for 50 years surveyor to Lloyd's, at Gloucester. He was a Liberal in politics all his life, and took a leading part in local politics. He also took a great interest in the Gloucester British Schools. He was a great friend of the working classes, and it was mainly through his instrumentality that the law relating to the capture of elvers was recently altered. The deceased was a brother to the late Mr. Francillon, Judge of the Gloucester County Court. He was widely known and much respected in Gloucester and the neighbourhood.

Appendix 1: John George Francillon Obituary,
Gloucester Journal July 9th 1881

Appendix 2:
Nine miles up the road, The Tewkesbury Register May 13th 1876 reported on what turned out to be the final prosecutions. Bailiff Huxley (who else)? In the company of two policemen on the night of April 25th summonsed James Stokes, George Reed, and Samuel Allen-alias Jones, at Deerhurst with illegally taking elvers.

The defendants stated that Huxley was so drunk, they had to take hold of him to prevent him from falling in the water. Also for the first time - the charge of aiding and abetting was brought against two of the accused:

Stokes	fined 5s & 6s. 6d costs.
Reed	fined 6s 6d costs. Aiding & Abetting
Allen alias (Jones)	fined 6s 6d costs. Aiding & Abetting

Thomas Roberts was convicted separately of illegal elvering at Deerhurst

Roberts	fined 5s & 9s costs.

My thanks to both Gloucester and Worcester record offices, and also CEFAS and English Heritage (National Monuments) - for permission to access and publish the sources listed below. Thanks again.